WE TAKE CARE OF OUR WORLD

by

Alex Hall

Minneapolis, Minnesota

Credits
Images are courtesy of Shutterstock.com. With thanks to Getty Images, Adobe Stock, Thinkstock Photo, and iStockphoto. Cover – Sumala Chidchoi, america365, Barks. 2–3 – Lithiumphoto, lilett. 4–5 – Monkey Business Images, wee dezign, Your Local Llamacorn, lilett, Polina Tomtosova. 6–7 – George Trumpeter, Elena Efimova, lilett, Polina Tomtosova. 8–9 – Beas777, PARALAXIS, lilett, Sonium_art. 10–11 – nEwyyy, Mr.anaked, mhatzapa, lilett, Polina Tomtosova. 12–13 – Rich Carey, Anita Patterson Peppers, lilett, Polina Tomtosova. 14–15 – FamVeld, Dmytro Zinkevych, lilett, Polina Tomtosova. 16–17 – SewCreamStudio, Manyna, lilett, Polina Tomtosova, mhatzapa, Rudzhan. 18–19 – TR STOK, Wichudapa, Dasha Rosato, Sonium_art, lilett, Polina Tomtosova. 20–21 – Ha-nu-man, Monkey Business Images, Bohdan Malitskiy, mhatzapa, lilett, Polina Tomtosova. 22–23 – WorldStockStudio, Jacob Lund, Rudzhan, lilett, Polina Tomtosova. 24 – lilett, Polina Tomtosova.

Bearport Publishing Company Product Development Team
Publisher: Jen Jenson; Director of Product Development: Spencer Brinker; Editorial Director: Allison Juda; Editor: Cole Nelson; Editor: Tiana Tran; Production Editor: Naomi Reich; Art Director: Kim Jones; Designer: Kayla Eggert; Designer: Steve Scheluchin; Production Specialist: Owen Hamlin

Library of Congress Cataloging-in-Publication Data is available at www.loc.gov or upon request from the publisher.

ISBN: 979-8-89577-029-0 (hardcover)
ISBN: 979-8-89577-460-1 (paperback)
ISBN: 979-8-89577-146-4 (ebook)

© 2026 BookLife Publishing
This edition is published by arrangement with BookLife Publishing.

North American adaptations © 2026 Bearport Publishing Company. All rights reserved. No part of this publication may be reproduced in whole or in part, stored in any retrieval system, or transmitted in any form or by any means, electronic, mechanical, photocopying, recording, or otherwise, without written permission from the publisher. Bearport Publishing is a division of FlutterBee Education Group.

For more information, write to Bearport Publishing, 3500 American Blvd W, Suite 150, Bloomington, MN 55431.

CONTENTS

WE ARE CONNECTED 4
CARING FOR OUR WORLD 6
TAKING FROM NATURE. 8
POLLUTING THE PLANET 10
CARING FOR ANIMALS 12
CARING FOR PLANTS 14
REDUCE, REUSE, RECYCLE 16
REDUCING AIR POLLUTION 18
HELPING FROM HOME 20
WHY IT IS GOOD TO TAKE CARE OF OUR WORLD . . . 22
GLOSSARY 24
INDEX 24

WE ARE CONNECTED

The world is full of people. We are all connected in a society. Together, we can make sure everyone has what they need.

There are more than 8 billion people in the world.

WHAT COMMUNITIES ARE YOU PART OF?

Within our society there are many different communities. These are groups that share things in common. Some communities are connected by a shared hometown or religion. But there are also communities formed by people who all like the same thing.

CARING FOR OUR WORLD

We all live together on Earth! This wonderful planet gives us everything we need to **survive**. We get air, water, and food from our world.

The natural space where plants and animals live is their **environment**.

How does Earth take care of you?

We only get one planet. So, we need to look after it. How can we take care of our world?

TAKING FROM NATURE

The planet is full of many **natural resources**. These are things made by Earth that we use in our daily lives. However, taking too much from nature can cause problems.

Wood, water, and soil are all natural resources.

We dig into the ground to find some resources. This is called mining.

When we remove resources, we take them away from an environment. This may make it harder for the plants and animals there to survive.

POLLUTING THE PLANET

Our planet is also being damaged by **pollution**. We add dangerous gases to the air when we burn **fuels** to power our factories and run our cars. This can be harmful to breathe.

Litter from land often ends up in the ocean.

Trash in places where it does not belong is another form of pollution. The land and water are full of litter. This can hurt an environment.

CARING FOR ANIMALS

Animals are often at risk when humans harm Earth. Wild homes are damaged when we take natural resources. Pollution can make animals sick.

Cutting down most of the trees in an area is called deforestation (dee-*for*-i-STAY-shuhn).

Part of caring for Earth is taking care of the animals on the planet. Keep their environments clean. Be kind to pets, and give any wild animals you see their space.

CARING FOR PLANTS

To stay healthy, environments also need plants. Plants clean our air. They also let out the **oxygen** animals need to breathe. Some animals eat plants to survive.

Working as a group makes caring for plants easier.

For years, humans have removed plants to make room for roads and towns. But we can help fix this. Plant trees to replace the ones that have been ripped up.

REDUCE, REUSE, RECYCLE

One way to help the planet is to make less trash. You can reduce, reuse, and recycle your things. Reducing means using less. This takes up fewer resources.

You can reuse the things you already have instead of getting something new.

Donating things you no longer need lets someone else use them.

16

WHAT DO YOU RECYCLE?

Recycling is a way to turn old things into something new again. Papers, plastics, glass, and metals can all be recycled.

REDUCING AIR POLLUTION

Driving cars and flying planes creates a lot of air pollution. This hurts all life on Earth. What can we do instead?

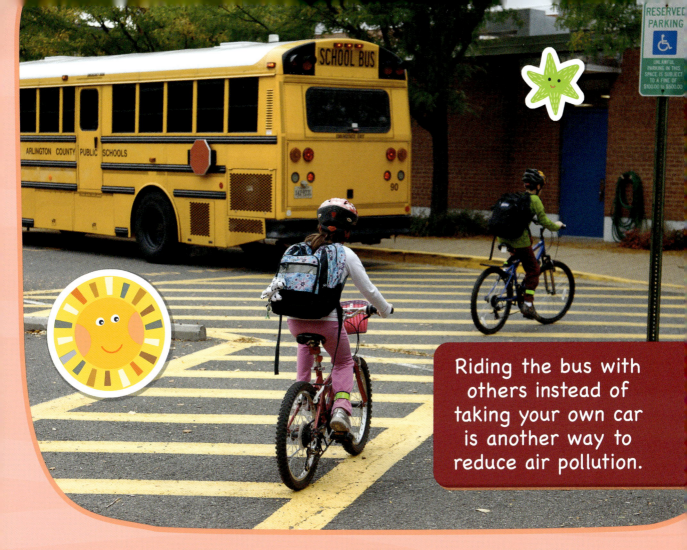

Riding the bus with others instead of taking your own car is another way to reduce air pollution.

When it is safe to do so, try riding your bike or walking. These ways of getting around don't make any air pollution. Plus, they are good for you!

HELPING FROM HOME

There are even things we can do at home to help the planet. Making the power for our homes creates air pollution. Using less power is better for Earth. Turn off the lights when you leave a room.

A FACTORY MAKING POWER

WHAT ARE OTHER WAYS YOU CAN USE LESS POWER AND WATER?

SAVE WATER

Water is a natural resource. Be sure not to waste it. Try taking short showers instead of baths. Remember to turn off the tap while brushing your teeth.

21

WHY IT IS GOOD TO TAKE CARE OF OUR WORLD

There are many ways to take care of our world. And a healthy Earth means all of the plants, people, and other animals on it are healthier, too.

What kind of society do you want to be part of?

Looking after our world works best when we all do our part. It takes teamwork. This makes our society a nice place to be. It is better when we are all connected!

GLOSSARY

communities groups of people who live together or shares something in common

environment the natural world where plants, animals, and people live

fuels things that are burned to produce heat or power

litter trash that has been left where it does not belong

natural resources useful things found in nature that people use or need

oxygen a gas in the air that animals need to survive

pollution anything that makes something unhealthy or dirty

survive to stay alive

INDEX

animals 6, 9, 12–14, 22
environment 6, 9, 11, 13–14
humans 12, 15
natural resources 8, 12, 21
plants 6, 9, 14–15, 22
pollution 10–12, 18–20
power 10, 20–21
recycle 16–17
reduce 16, 18–19
reuse 16
water 6, 8, 11, 21